Helping Children See Jesus

ISBN: 978-1-933206-52-3

Rainbow Garden
Based on Rainbow Garden by Patricia St. John

Adaptation: Rose-Mae Carvin
Cover Illustration: Kathy Harmon   Illustrator: Frances Hertzler
Typesetting and Layout: Morgan Melton, Patricia Pope

© 1960 by Patricia St. John
Scripture Union USA: PO Box 215, Valley Forge, PA 19481
CANADA: 1885 Clements Road Unit 226, Pickering ON L1W 3V4

© 2019 Bible Visuals International
PO Box 153, Akron, PA 17501-0153
Phone: (717) 859-1131
www.biblevisuals.org

All rights reserved. No part of this publication may be reproduced, stored in a retrieval system or transmitted in any form by any means, electronic, mechanical, photocopy, recording or otherwise, without the prior permission of the publisher, except as provided by USA copyright law. Published by Scripture Union in England and used by arrangement with them

RELATED ITEMS

To access related items (such as activities, memory verse posters and translated texts) please visit our web store at shop.biblevisuals.org and enter 5500 in the search box on the page.

FREE TEXT DOWNLOAD

To access a FREE printable copy of the teaching text (PDF format) in English or other available languages, enter S5500DL in the search box. Add the item to your cart, and use coupon code XTACSV17 at checkout. Once your order is processed you will receive an email with a link to the free download.

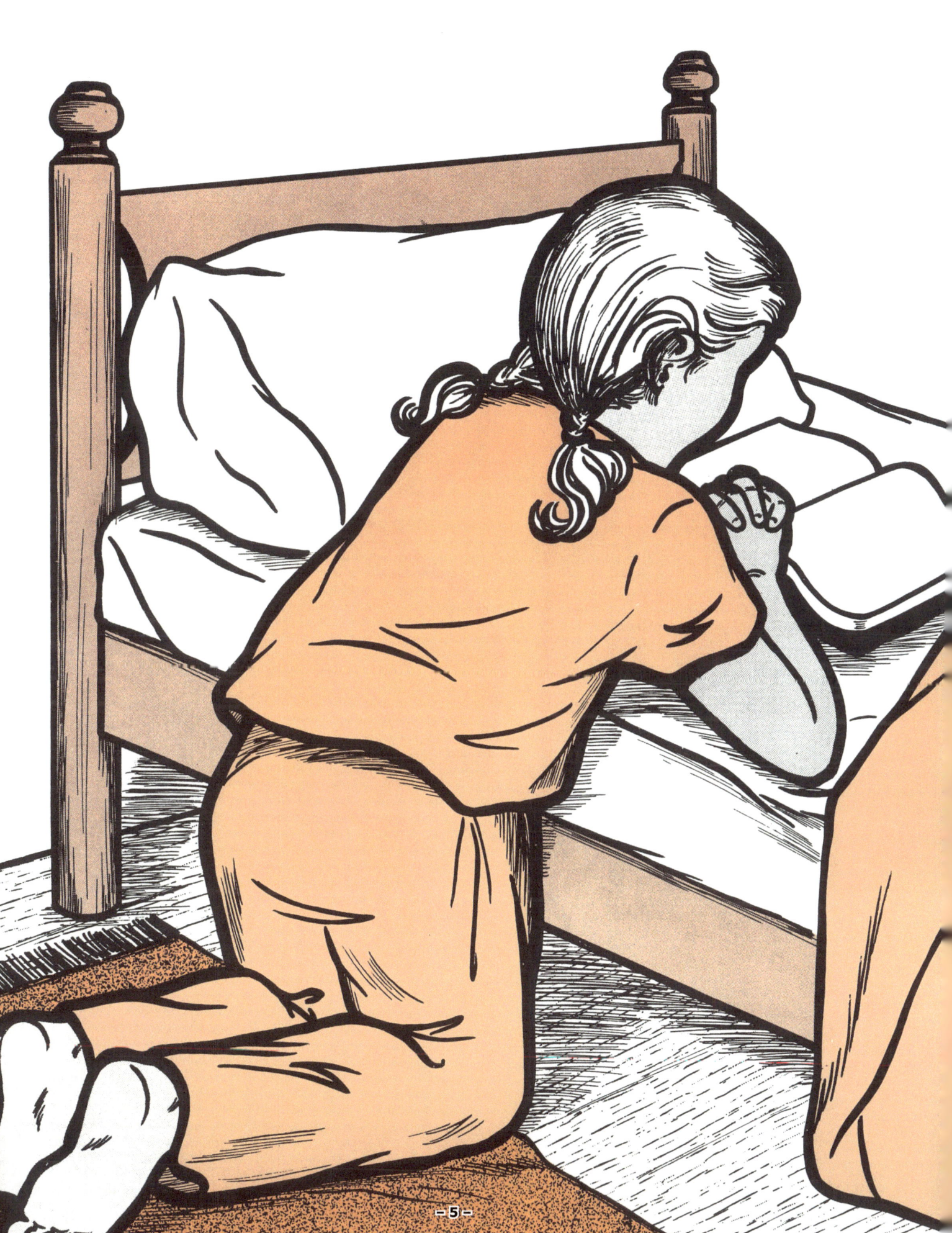

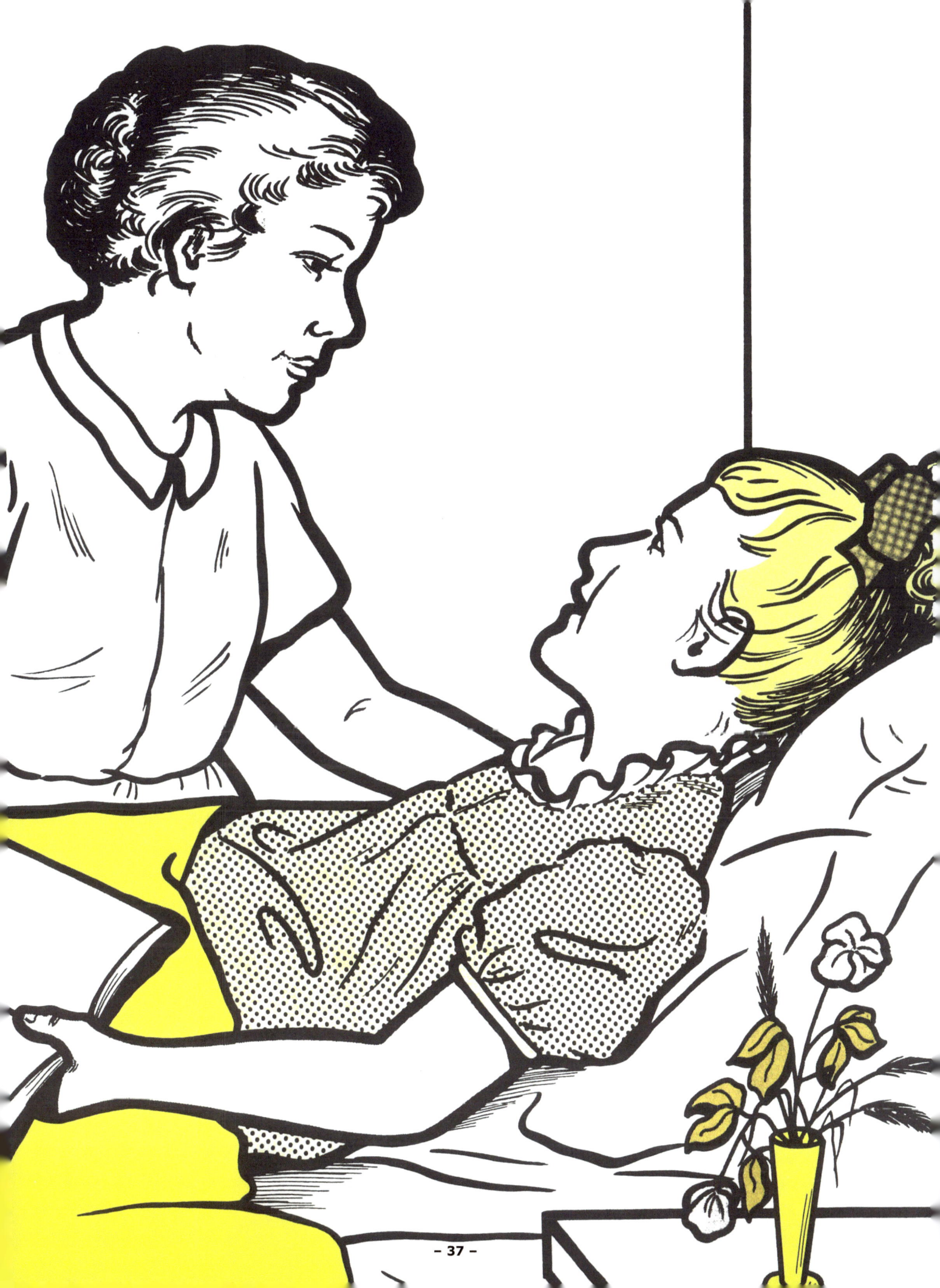

WELCOME HOME

Thou wilt shew me the path of life: in Thy presence is fulness of joy; at Thy right hand there are pleasures for evermore. Psalm 16:11

© Bible Visuals International Inc

Chapter 1

Show Illustration #1

Elaine sat at the table with a puzzled frown on her face. She had seen a Bible in the church she sometimes attended in the big city. But never before had she seen one on the supper table. Surely the father was not going to read from that dull, uninteresting book while all the family sat at the table and listened. But this is exactly what the father did.

What kind of place is this my mother has sent me to? Elaine thought. *It is bad enough leaving the big city to live in this awful lonely country with its big, open spaces without having to live with a foolish family. Well, I just won't listen!*

Instead of listening to the Bible reading, Elaine studied each member of this family where she was to live for at least a year while her mother went to Europe.

There was Mr. Owen, the father, a tall man with kind eyes. And Mrs. Owen, whose face always seemed to be smiling. Her eyes were dark and her hair curly. *How can she smile with all these children to take care of?* Elaine wondered.

Around the table sat Peter the oldest, and Janet who was ten and just a few months younger than Elaine. Next came the three little steps, Johnny and Frances and Robin, each just a wee bit taller than the other. In her carriage close by lay baby Lucy, blue-eyed and dimpled. To Elaine, who never had lived with other children, this large family was terrifying. And the big, ugly dog who tried to make friends with her–he was the most frightening thing about the whole place!

Mr. Owen went on reading the Bible and Elaine finally realized he was reading something about a vine and its branches. Then the last verse caught her attention: "These things have I spoken unto you . . . that your joy might be full."

Elaine liked the sound of those words. She repeated them over and over in her mind as the family bowed their heads and Mr. Owen prayed.

Of all the silly things, thought Elaine. *Praying is for churches, not for tables. It is a good idea to say the Lord's Prayer before going to sleep at night. But this is very silly.*

Show Illustration #2

Yet Elaine observed that Mr. Owen was not praying as the minister did in church. This was different. Mr. Owen prayed as if he knew God very well–as if God was right there. It was all very puzzling to the little girl from the big city who had come to live with this family in the country. She was glad when the Bible reading and prayer were finished.

"Did you enjoy family worship?" Janet asked. Without waiting for an answer she continued, "I'll show you where you are to sleep, Elaine. You and I are to share my room. Won't that be fun?"

Elaine did not think this would be fun at all. She was used to having her own room all to herself. In fact she was used to having almost everything to herself. She knew little about sharing anything. Elaine was a very selfish little girl.

When Janet led Elaine into the room they were to share, Elaine said nothing. Yet her face showed only too well how awful she thought it was. True, everything was clean and neat. But it was not at all like the frilly little room she had in the city.

Show Illustration #3

When she saw some sticky candy and withered flowers on her pillow she snatched them and tossed them in the waste basket.

Janet shot an angry glance at Elaine. "I am glad my little sister didn't see you do that," she said, her voice shaking. "She wanted to do something nice for you and make you feel you were welcome. Now I am not so sure you are." And Janet ran quickly from the room.

Elaine looked surprised. She thought the candy and flowers were trash someone had carelessly left on her pillow. She was thoughtless and selfish. But she was not cruel. *Which one of the little sisters was it?* she thought. *I hope she doesn't find out about this.*

Show Illustration #4

Then Elaine shrugged her shoulders, undressed and crept into her bed. For a long time she lay awake thinking about the day and about her new home. *How could Mother ever have gone off and left me to stay in this shabby place with this crowd of children for one whole year? I'll be expected to share and I'll be expected to help with the work, I'm sure. Well I won't do it! I'll do as I please just as I've always done. Tomorrow I'll demand a room of my own. I won't have Janet's dull dresses crowding my lovely, bright ones in this tiny closet. And I know I won't sleep a wink all night with Janet sleeping in the same room.*

When Elaine heard Janet coming to bed, she closed her eyes and lay very still, pretending to be asleep. Every once in a while she peeked from under lowered lashes and watched Janet.

Janet looked at the pile of clothes Elaine had left lying on the floor where she had undressed. For a moment an angry look crossed her face. Then she glanced at Elaine and shook her head. "Poor girl," she murmured as she picked up the clothing and hung it neatly in the closet. Elaine felt a little twinge of shame.

But what was this Janet was doing? Not reading more of the Bible, surely? Couldn't they ever get enough of the Bible?

Show Illustration #5

When Janet knelt beside her bed Elaine sat up and watched. Janet's lips were moving quietly but Elaine heard her whisper, "Bless Elaine and help us to help her to be happy and to come to know You."

Anger filled Elaine's heart. This was the end! *Tomorrow,* she thought, *I'll tell that goody-goody Janet that she doesn't need to pray for me. If things are going to be like this around here, I might have to run away. Then Mother will be sorry she left me here. She'd blame the Owens for letting me leave. I'll show them!*

Elaine turned her eyes to the window. The sky was filled with stars. It seemed like such a wide, wide sky without high roofs and spires crowding each other against it. How she missed the city–and her own little room. She was a very unhappy, homesick girl.

And then, just before she finally fell asleep, the words Mr. Owen had read from the Bible came to her mind again: "These things have I spoken unto you, that your joy might be full."

What things? Elaine wondered.

She wished now that she had listened to the rest of the Bible reading. Perhaps Mr. Owen would read it again sometime. And Elaine, the poor girl who had only the things money can buy, fell asleep on a pillow wet with her tears.

If only Elaine could have known what a fortunate girl she was to have come to live with a Christian family who knew and loved the Lord!

Chapter 2

The day after Elaine arrived to live with the Owen family was Sunday. She expected to be able to sleep late as she usually did on Sunday mornings when she lived with her mother.

It seemed very early to the city girl when Janet stood beside her bed and said, "Come, Elaine, it's time to get up. We don't want to be late for church."

Elaine sat up quickly and looked closely at Janet. It appeared that Janet was no longer angry. Elaine hoped Janet would forget about the candy and withered flowers which she had thrown in the waste basket.

But as they sat down to breakfast, little Frances leaned over and whispered in Elaine's ear, "Did you get them? Did you like them?"

"Get what? Like what?" Elaine answered.

"Why the candy, of course. And the flowers. You did find them on your pillow, didn't you?"

"Oh, those! Yes, I found them, thank you."

Frances' little face showed her disappointment.

The Owen family took up one whole pew in the church. They all turned to smile at friends in other pews as they filed in and sat down–that is all except Elaine. She felt that everyone was staring at her. She kept her eyes to the floor.

'Spose they think I'm some orphan girl the Owens have taken in, she thought. *I'll soon let them know I'm richer than any of them–and better too. I won't speak to any of them.*

When the service was over, Elaine walked as quickly as she could down the aisle and outside. She hurried around to the back of the church where she would not be seen. Suddenly she realized she was standing in an old cemetery. Idly she glanced at the tombstones on the graves.

Show Illustration #6

She read words carved on one of the tombstones, "David Davies–1710-1780." *My, but he has been dead for a long time,* Elaine thought. At the bottom of the tombstone she read, "In . . . The next words were completely worn away. With great difficulty she read the last words, "fullness of joy." Her heart missed a beat. *This sounds something like the words Mr. Owen read at family worship. Only this sounds even better. But what can the missing words be? "In" where is "fullness of joy"?*

It rained most of the day. Yet Elaine discovered that the Owens expected to go again to the church for Sunday school in the afternoon. *How tiresome!* she thought. *How terribly, terribly tiresome!*

There was free time after dinner, she discovered, when one might do as she pleased. The other children were reading or playing games. Elaine started to write a letter to her mother. Where she sat she could glance out the window. She did more glancing than writing, and soon she saw the sun shining through the raindrops.

Show Illustration #7

And there was a rainbow–the brightest, most beautiful rainbow Elaine had ever seen. No one else seemed to see it.

Quietly, so as not to disturb the others, Elaine walked from the room. This was *her* rainbow and she was not going to share it if she could help it. She got her raincoat from the hallway and slipped out of the house.

Elaine had heard stories about treasures being hidden at the ends of rainbows; and the end of this rainbow was just up the hill. It seemed to touch the earth behind an old stone wall.

When Elaine reached the stone wall it looked as if the rainbow must be inside. But the wall was high and seemed to enclose a house and garden. The wall had ivy hanging over it like curtains and it looked secret and exciting.

Elaine saw a wooden gate. But when she tried to open it, she found it was locked. Pressing her face close, she looked through the cracks. There was indeed a house inside–a house with all the shades pulled down. Surely no one lived in it.

Elaine climbed over the gate and stood all out of breath on the other side, looking at a garden which would have been very lovely had it not been overgrown with weeds. The rainbow was not there now but Elaine was sure the end of it must have rested lightly on the big clump of white flowers which she thought were called snow-drops.

Show Illustration #8

The house was quite empty. Of this she was certain. The windows were all locked and darkened. Great dusty cobwebs clung to the front door. Surely no one had lived here in a long time.

"This is going to be MY garden," Elaine spoke out loud. "No one else will ever come in here. This is where I'll hide when I want to get away from all those awful Owen children."

Show Illustration #9

And then Elaine stood very still. She was too frightened to move. She saw a man climbing over the garden gate. He did not see her until he was close to the house.

Elaine thought the man too was frightened. But after a moment he said in a pleasant voice, "How do you do? Is there anyone at home?"

"I don't think so." Elaine's voice shook. "I think it's an empty house. Either no one lives here, or they have all gone away."

"Then what are you doing here?" This time the man scowled and his voice was not pleasant.

Elaine hesitated for a moment. Then she said, "Oh, I take care of the garden."

"Oh you do, eh?" The man gave a funny little laugh as he glanced at the weeds growing all around. "Come here every day?"

"Oh no," Elaine replied. "I only come Saturdays and Sundays. That is, I will be coming on Saturdays and Sundays. I haven't started to take care of the garden yet. I've just come to live with the Owens and of course I'll be going to school on weekdays. But on Saturdays and Sundays I'll take care of the garden. I have been hired to do it."

Never for a moment did Elaine hesitate when a lie would help her out. A lie never bothered her at all, unless of course she got caught in one.

"Well, if there is no one at home, there is no use staying longer," and the man walked back to the gate and climbed over it as he had entered.

Elaine noticed how pale the man was, even though his face was covered with whiskers. It looked as if it had been a long time since he had shaved. His clothes were wrinkled and dirty and he smelled of whiskey. She noticed how he pulled his cap down over his evil eyes before he went away. How glad she was when he had gone!

Elaine's legs were so weak with fright that she had a hard time climbing back over the gate. But when she got back to the house she managed to let Mrs. Owen think she had only been out walking.

"Where have you been, Elaine? The others have gone off to Sunday school. I was about to come look for you."

Show Illustration #10

"Please, Mrs. Owen," Elaine said. "I found a secret place where I'd like to go alone sometimes. Please may I? And not let the others know where it is? It's just around the corner on the other side of those bushes."

Mrs. Owen knew about "secret places" which boys and girls liked to try to keep from others. It was always fun if they could succeed. "Why, of course, Elaine. Only please be sure you let me know when you go so I won't be worried."

Chapter 3

Show Illustration #11

Elaine listened a little more carefully when Mr. Owen read the Bible at family worship that evening. She was listening for the verse about fullness of joy. But she was too proud to ask about it.

Each of the members of the family prayed after the Bible reading but no one seemed to expect Elaine to do so. She felt as if she had been left out and made up her mind that next time she would pray too. She could find something to say whether she meant it or not. They needn't think they were so smart!

The family sat and talked for a while. Sunday was the day for these family get-togethers. Each child could tell something of interest which happened that day, or during the week.

Show Illustration #12

"I'd like to tell about some lambs," Janet said.

"Peter and I went to help Mr. Jones with his sheep one day this week. Just before we got there one of the mother sheep had two baby lambs."

"Really?" Mrs. Owen said.

Yes, Mr. Jones was surprised and pleased. But one little lamb died as soon as it was born." All the children said, "A-a-ah, too bad."

"Yes, but listen," Janet continued. "A little while before this, a mother sheep had died right after her one baby lamb was born. And do you know what Mr. Jones did? He skinned the dead baby lamb and wrapped that skin around the little orphan lamb. Then he took it to the mother whose one baby had died. She sniffed at the wool, thought it was her own lamb, and let it feed with the other!"

Turning towards Peter, Janet said, "You tell about the little lamb that really belonged to the mother, Peter. After all, you saw it, too."

Peter had been finding it hard to keep quiet and was glad for a chance to talk.

Show Illustration #13

"Well, do you know what?" he asked excitedly. "That brand new baby lamb was not fooled, even though the mother was. It did not want to share its dinner with another and it kept butting and butting the new lamb. You might think it had its horns already."

When everyone laughed at this, Peter continued, "Mr. Jones said we were to leave the lambs alone. He said the new one was larger and would have to learn to make his own way. But Janet and I felt sorry for the lamb. It just cried when the other lamb butted it. We were afraid it would starve."

Janet's eyes were shining. "You finish, Jan," Peter said.

"Well, when we went there a day or two later, guess what? There was that new lamb feeding along with the other one. He even butted a little himself when the other one took up too much room."

Elaine found herself joining in the laughter with a warm little feeling inside.

Then Mrs. Owen spoke quietly. "The lambs remind us of people, don't they?" she asked.

"How, Mother?" they all wanted to know.

"Well, there are times when we can fool other Christians into thinking we are Christians, when we really never have been born again. Sometimes we may even become angry, like the little lamb and try to 'butt' those who doubt us. All this is possible. But we can never fool God. He always knows whether we really belong to Him or not."

Elaine thought, *A few moments ago I had planned to pray as the others did, just to prove I could. I was like the little lamb dressed up in false wool. I really do not belong to God.*

Then it was little Frances' turn to talk. She wanted to tell what she had learned in Sunday school. Tossing back her lovely curls she straightened her dress, sat up tall, cleared her throat, and began:

"It was like this. God told Cain and Mabel to bring a lamb." Francie's voice was very solemn. The deep dimple in one cheek went in and out as she spoke and her eyes were big and round. Elaine found herself liking this little girl. Francie continued, "But Cain brought vegubbles. But God didn't want vegubbles. And Cain gave Mabel a great big push and he fell down dead– and after that Cain was dreffully busy because he had to look after all Mabel's lambs as well as his own vegubbles."

It was plain to see how difficult it was for everyone to keep from laughing at little Francie's version of the story of Cain and Abel. But they all loved their little sister dearly and none of them would hurt her feelings.

Show Illustration #14

It was Janet who put her arms around little Frances and said, "Little sister, your story needs a few things sort of 'fixed up.' Suppose we go over it together before you get into bed tonight, shall we?"

Mr. Owen glanced at his older daughter with deep love in his eyes. As for Elaine, she wondered what it was that needed to be "fixed up." For she was more ignorant than little Francie of the real story. She began to realize there were many things she did not know.

Two tired girls went to bed that night. Again Elaine pretended to be asleep. But secretly she watched Janet as she knelt in prayer. In her heart, Elaine wished she could be more like Janet.

After Janet was in bed and the room was dark, Elaine spoke. "Janet do you know what 'fullness of joy' means?"

Janet was surprised. "What do you mean, 'fullness of joy,' Elaine?"

"Well, I thought you knew some Bible verses. I know the beginning of the verse and I know the end, but I don't know the middle. It's like this: IN something *IS FULNESS OF JOY.* I'd like to know, in *what* is 'fullness of joy'?"

"W-e-l-l," Janet did not like to admit she was not sure. "I think it is 'in heaven is fullness of joy.' Yes I'm sure that's it."

Elaine paused for a moment. Then, because she found it easier to talk in the darkness, she asked what had been wrong about little Francie's story of Cain and Mabel.

Janet explained how it was really Cain and Abel, not Mabel.

Show Illustration #15

She told Elaine how Cain had wanted to bring God his own kind of offering. But Abel was obedient and brought a lamb as an offering, according to the command of God.

"Then Cain was angry and he killed his brother Abel and became the first murderer in the world. You see, Elaine, we can't expect to do things our way. We must do as God says. Mother says if we truly belong to God's family we will want to obey Him. We won't be wanting our own way all the time."

Elaine lay a long time after Janet was peacefully sleeping. There was much to be learned about God and the Bible. She began to see that she was very ignorant about such things.

Elaine started to look forward to family worship where she would learn from the Bible. She still did not quite understand about "fullness of joy."

Chapter 4

Elaine could scarcely wait for the week to pass so she could hide away again by herself. Each time it rained she looked for a rainbow to arch right into her garden, as it had the day she discovered it.

Saturday was a nice sunny day. Although there seemed little hope for a rainbow, Elaine watched her chance to slip away when the other children were busy.

Show Illustration #16

She whispered to Mrs. Owen, "I am going to you-know-where."

Mrs. Owen nodded and gave Elaine a smile and a little wink.

Elaine climbed over the wooden gate and glanced around her garden. A week of much sunshine following the soft rain had brought out some lovely flowers. Yellow daffodils were in a golden ring around the chestnut tree which had tiny new leaves. Tulip leaves were pushing up through the earth and birds were singing. To Elaine they seemed to be singing, "Fullness of joy! Fullness of joy!"

As Elaine watched, a bird with a brown and white speckled breast darted from the lilac bush. Janet and Peter had taught Elaine that this could mean there was a nest close by. Parting the boughs Elaine peeped in. Yes, there was a nest, carefully woven from twigs and moss and mud. And down at the bottom of it lay two turquoise eggs speckled with black markings.

"Another lovely secret," Elaine murmured. "All my own. I won't share it."

Elaine was looking forward to a wonderful time all alone. She had not been quite truthful with Mrs. Owen about her secret place being a garden. She felt sure no one would be able to find her here.

And then Elaine noticed something different about the house. The front door was closed as before and the vines and cobwebs still clung to it. But the window closest to the front door had been broken. There was a big open space and the curtains had been taken away.

Carefully Elaine pulled herself up to the low window sill. There was plenty of room for a little girl to craw through. And crawl through she did, her heart pounding with excitement.

Show Illustration #17

How surprised she was to find every thing in the house in a terrible mess! Whoever lived here seemed to be most untidy. Chests of drawers were open and everything was spilled out on the floor.

With heart thumping Elaine went slowly up the wide stairs to the bedrooms. Here everything was in the same condition. Drawers were open and clothing was scattered all over the floor.

But the last bedroom Elaine peeped into was still in order. It was a little girl's room. Of this Elaine was certain when she saw some dolls on a cot and doll furniture in a lovely doll house. Whoever lived here surely had a little girl. Elaine wondered where they were and if they would be coming back here to live. And who had broken that window? Then Elaine remembered the dirty-looking man who had been in the garden the week before. Frightened, she hurried down the stairs.

As she passed through the long hall downstairs Elaine noticed a cabinet filled with lovely shells. She stopped to look at them. One was very large and very beautiful. *Peter would surely like this for his collection,* Elaine thought. Without stopping to think further, she quickly picked up the shell, climbed out of the window, ran through the garden, and over the gate.

Hurrying along the path toward the house, Elaine planned what she would do with the shell. *Those smarty kids are always finding shells for Peter's collection,* she thought. *None of them ever found one like this. What will they think of me now?*

When she reached the house, Elaine carried her shell carefully.

Show Illustration #18

She found Peter and Janet busy arranging the shells. "See what I have found for your collection, Peter?" Elaine's cheeks were red with excitement.

Peter and Janet looked at her strangely.

"Do you mean you've been down beside the sea in such a short time?" Janet wanted to know.

"I can run fast when I want to," Elaine pouted.

"But, Elaine, you never found a shell like this beside *our* sea," Peter said. "There are no shells this large around here."

Angrily Elaine shouted, "You are just the meanest, most selfish children I've ever known! You never want me to go with you when you go to find shells because you think I am only in the way. And when I do find one bigger and better than you ever found, you say I didn't find it. Where do you think I got it, if I didn't find it, I'd like to know?"

Elaine was about to storm out of the house again. Peter took hold of her arm. "I didn't say you didn't find it." He shook her a little. "But I do say such shells aren't found around here and it must have been washed miles and miles from some other coast. I'm very glad to have it, Elaine. Thank you."

None of the children had noticed Mr. Owen standing in the doorway. Now he walked into the room. "May I see this shell, please?" he said in a quiet voice.

Elaine scarcely breathed as Mr. Owen examined the shell. "Very lovely," he said. "First it looks pink, then green, and then sort of a mixture of the two."

"I've seen a shell like this in Philippa's cabinet," Janet said.

Elaine wheeled around. "Who is Philippa?" she wanted to know. She didn't notice the strange look on Mr. Owen's face as he watched her.

"Haven't we told you? Philippa is the girl who lives up the hill. She is lame and can't walk. Her mother took her to the city to see some doctors who think they may help her. Haven't you noticed the house with the stone wall around it and the garden in front?"

So the little girl who owned the lovely dolls was called Philippa! *Would she miss her shell?* Elaine wondered.

Show Illustration #19

That night at family worship, Mr. Owen read from the third chapter of Genesis, about the disobedience of Adam and Eve and how God had to turn them out of their lovely garden never to return. Mr. Owen explained that they had been happy in the garden–not just because it was beautiful, but because God was with them. But their sin separated them from God and then there was nothing but sadness.

Elaine lay awake that night thinking about the Bible reading. It seemed to her drowsy mind that it must have been written about her and her garden. She knew it would never be beautiful and happy and peaceful because of what she had done. Perhaps somehow God had been waiting for her among the flowers, waiting to make her happy like Adam and Eve. But her sin had spoiled it all.

And she could not go back now to see the little eggs hatch, nor to hear the birds sing, "Fullness of joy–fullness of joy."

She buried her face in her pillow and cried.

The door opened quietly and Mrs. Owen gathered the weeping girl in her arms. Elaine sobbed and sobbed, clinging closely to the woman. But she would not tell the cause of her tears.

Chapter 5

The days which followed were extremely unhappy for Elaine. She could not look forward to visiting her little garden. *That is all past and gone,* she thought. And she dreaded the day when Philippa would come home. She told no one about the open window. She was afraid her theft and lying might be found out. To make things worse, there was a week's vacation from school. And what could an unhappy, guilty girl do with a whole week?

Elaine sat thinking about this as the other children made vacation plans. They didn't seem to notice that Elaine did not enter into their plans.

Show Illustration #20

Suddenly Peter yelled, "Hey! There's a policeman coming to our door. I wonder what he wants. Do you suppose the dog has killed another chicken?"

Everyone crowded to the window to look at the policeman–everyone except Elaine. No one saw her dash out the back door. She had a queer, sick feeling inside. She was certain the policeman was after her. Someone must have seen the broken window and missing shell, and reported having seen her around there. *Will they put me in jail?* Elaine wondered.

She ran up the hill as fast as her trembling legs would carry her. She didn't know where she was going, but she knew she was *not* going to Philippa's house and the little garden.

Elaine darted through the sheep pasture. The frightened lambs ran out of her way as she dashed on and on! Elaine had forgotten she could be seen from the back of the Owen's house. Nor did she know that Mr. Owen was watching her as she ran–watched until he saw her enter the woods–before he went into the room where the policeman was questioning the family.

Show Illustration #21

Elaine reached a little clearing in the woods where someone had made a pile of logs. There she sat and tried to think what to do. She did not dare to go too far into the woods. And yet she was afraid to go back. If they sent her to prison, what would her mother think? And those stuck-up Owen children who never told lies nor stole! She could not bear to think of the looks on their faces. And so she sat and cried. Instead of feeling sorry for what she had done, she was feeling sorry for herself. "Oh, why, why, did my mother ever send me to this horrid place?" she wailed.

And then Elaine heard the bark of a dog and the sound of feet coming towards her. She sat as if she were frozen to the log, not daring to move. *It must be the police,* she thought, *and they have their dogs hunting for me!*

The frightened girl gave a little scream and then there was a dog indeed. But he was wagging his tail and licking her face. It was the Owen's dog. Behind him came Mr. Owen. Now Elaine sobbed and sobbed and Mr. Owen sat down beside her and put his arm around her.

Show Illustration #22

"Why did you run away, Elaine? Were you frightened of that policeman? He only wanted to ask you a few questions. You see, there has been a robbery in the house where Philippa lives. And the policeman thought perhaps you children might have seen someone hanging around there when you were out playing."

And then Elaine found herself telling Mr. Owen the whole story of her garden, the smelly man, the open window, and the shell. Somehow it was easy to talk to him out here in the woods, as she snuggled between Mr. Owen and the big, warm dog.

"You'll be able to be a big help to the police, Elaine, since you had a good look at the man and can describe him. You need not tell them about the shell. You and I can deal with that shell between us. You took it because you wanted the others to think you'd found something nice for Peter's collection. And you said you'd found it on the beach?"

"Yes," Elaine whispered.

"Did it make you happy?"

Elaine shook her head. "I kept being afraid you'd find out."

"That wasn't the only reason you were unhappy, Elaine. You were unhappy because you had stolen and told a lie. Sin always makes us unhappy. Do you remember hearing about Adam and Eve at family worship?"

Elaine nodded.

"Well, you were happy in your garden until you sinned. Sin always makes us unhappy because it separates us from God. It was for sin that the Lord Jesus came to this earth. When He hung on the cross He took upon Himself the sin that was between us and God. *He* was punished for it, instead of us. Now the way is open for us to come to God, asking His forgiveness and finding 'fullness of joy.'"

Elaine looked up quickly when she heard the familiar words, "fullness of joy."

"I know that verse," she said. "It is, 'In heaven is fullness of joy.' Janet taught it to me."

Mr. Owen smiled. "Then Janet taught you all wrong," he said. "It is far, far better than that. It's like this: 'Thou [God] wilt show me the path of life; in Thy presence is fullness of joy.' That means that anywhere in the world, if you are walking in the path of life close to God, you can be perfectly happy."

Show Illustration #23

And that day, out in the woods, Elaine asked the Lord Jesus to be her very own Saviour and forgive her sins. Mr. Owen read verses from the New Testament which he always carried in his pocket. It seemed to Elaine that a heavy burden was lifted from her young shoulders as she prayed, repeating the words after Mr. Owen:

"O Lord, I want to tell You about the shell I stole and the lies I told and all the things I was so afraid and unhappy about. I am coming to You because Jesus died. You promised to forgive. Please wash me whiter than snow and make me Your own girl. And come into my heart and make me brave and truthful, so I can make right what I did. For Jesus' sake, Amen."

As they walked home hand in hand, Mr. Owen said, "Let's tell them about it tonight at family worship, Elaine. You'll be much happier when it is all over and you can start again. And anyhow, it won't be as bad as you think. Peter and Janet have a lot to make right too, as I see it."

Elaine went to her bed that night happier than she had ever been in her short life. She wanted to ask Janet to help her to pray. So she stayed up, waiting for her.

But when Janet came in the room, Elaine saw she had been crying.

Show Illustration #24

Coming to sit on the side of Elaine's bed, Janet said, "Elaine, Daddy has been talking to Peter and me. He says we are largely to blame for you stealing the shell because of the way we treated you. We made you feel you were not as smart as we were. So you stole the shell to make us think you were smart, too. We are both sorry and Peter will tell you so tomorrow. I am asking you to forgive me, Elaine. And let's be real good friends."

If Elaine thought her day had ended happily before, she was certainly sure of it now as the girls pushed their beds close together and lay awake talking for a long time that night.

"I have found out what 'fullness of joy' means now, Janet," Elaine whispered. "It is to be in God's presence. I could not ever be there before because of my sin. But now I can and this is surely 'fullness of joy.' I am so glad now that my mother sent me to live with you and I don't ever want to go home again. And will you go with me when I put the shell back tomorrow, Janet? Well, will you?"

Raising up on her elbow, Elaine saw that Janet was fast asleep.

Smiling, Elaine turned on her side and in a moment, she too was asleep, a happy girl who now belonged to a new family– God's family.

Chapter 6

During the week of vacation which followed, Elaine had many new experiences with Peter and Janet. They were patient with her. And she was a willing learner. Shyly Peter told her he was sorry for the way he had treated her.

Elaine tried her best to keep up with Peter and Janet as they raced through the meadows, hunted for shells beside the sea, and looked for birds' nests. She took them to the little garden and showed them the nest she had discovered for herself a week or two before. "Well, why ever didn't you tell us about this?" Peter wanted to know.

Then Janet had an idea. "Philippa will be coming back the end of this week," she said. "Why don't we get this messy garden in order for her? Since she is lame now I think her mother will probably move her room downstairs and she can look right out on the garden."

Show Illustration #25

Busy days followed when Mr. Owen repaired the window and the children worked in the garden. This was much better than doing it alone, Elaine decided. She peeked in the window. It felt good to see the shell back in the cabinet where it belonged.

On the last morning everyone went up the hill to inspect the garden and took gifts they wanted to leave for Philippa. Peter had made a hutch in which he placed a little rabbit. Mr. Owen used the key he had been given to open the door so the other children could leave plates of home-made cookies and fudge. Little Francie put her favorite toy elephant on Philippa's bed, giving it a little pat as she left the room.

"Please may I stay a little longer?" Elaine pleaded when the others started home for dinner. "I haven't quite finished weeding this little spot around the lilac bush."

Mrs. Owen smiled. She understood. "Yes," she said, "you must finish your job, Elaine." Then whispering, "It will be nice for you to be alone in your little garden once more. Now you know that God is with you and you understand the little bird's song, 'Fullness of joy!'"

Elaine sat for a long time thinking and enjoying the garden flowers and the singing of the birds. She wondered what the little girl who lived here would be like. And would that evil man ever come again and frighten the lame girl? But she must do the weeding if she was to get home before dark.

And then, surprised, Elaine heard the squeal of brakes as an automobile came to a stop in front of the gate. She watched for a moment as a woman got out of the car and helped a frail girl get out.

Show Illustration #26

The girl walked slowly, using crutches. There were heavy braces on her legs. It was Philippa and her mother!

Elaine dashed around the corner of the house like a frightened rabbit and pressed herself against the wall. They might not like a stranger in their garden.

"Oh, Mother, look! The garden! It's all alive! And we thought it would be filled with weeds."

"Well, it's just as though fairies had been at work. How beautiful it looks! I am sure we have the Owens to thank for this. How kind they are!"

Philippa shouted. "Oh, look! There's a rabbit hutch around the side of the house. Come quick and see if there's a rabbit inside."

Show Illustration #27

Elaine flattened herself against the wall. But very soon two frightened girls stood looking at each other, not knowing what to say.

"What are you doing here?" Philippa's mother wanted to know.

"Nothing," Elaine stammered guiltily. "At least . . . I was gardening. Mrs. Owen said I could. I live with the Owens. We all came together to get ready for Philippa."

Philippa's mother burst out laughing. "Why you must be Elaine," she said, "the girl who saw our burglar. Mrs. Owen wrote and told us about you. We thank you very much for making the garden so beautiful. Please come inside so we can get acquainted."

That very day Elaine and Philippa became friends. Philippa wanted to know who made the cookies and the fudge. Tears came to her eyes when Elaine told her about Francie and the little elephant which was on Philippa's bed.

Show Illustration #28

After Elaine said goodbye to her new friend, she skipped all the way home just as the sun was setting. She felt as if she could spread wings and fly.

It's a funny thing, she thought, *but it's much more fun doing things for other people than just doing them for myself.*

Then, as she jumped over a clump of bushes, Elaine thought of Philippa lying on her bed, her small face pale and thin. *I must do all I can to help her to be happy. I wonder if Philippa knows about 'fullness of joy.' I wonder if she is in God's presence because she too has taken the Lord Jesus as her Saviour.*

As the family ate dinner, Elaine told them about being caught by Philippa and her mother when they arrived. They all laughed together.

Elaine looked forward to family worship now. She was getting fairly good at finding places in the old worn Bible the Owens had given her.

"I have a special reason to want to get to be good at this now," she said. "I want to try to show Philippa some things in here, if she doesn't already know them."

Then just before he started to read, Mr. Owen excused himself and left the room. When he returned he had a parcel in his hands which he handed to Elaine.

"For me?" Elaine asked in surprise.

"Yes, my dear, for you. If you are going to try to be good at finding places in the Bible you might as well start with this one."

Elaine's fingers trembled as she opened her gift. Tears filled her eyes as she read the inside front page:

ELAINE NELSON

"Thou wilt show me the path of life. In Thy presence is fullness of joy" (Psalm 16:11a).

She had come to know what the "fullness of joy" was. Perhaps the "path of life" for her was to help Philippa also find fullness of joy.

Chapter 7

School was over for the summer. Elaine spent many happy hours with her new-found friend, Philippa, who lay on a hammock in the garden. Elaine read to her from the new Bible, each time repeating what had been studied the evening before at the Owens' family worship.

Show Illustration #29

And then one day, with the late afternoon sun making a rosy glow about the little lame girl, she too bowed her head and found the fullness of joy which comes from knowing the Lord Jesus as Lord and Saviour.

Late that summer there was great excitement as the Owen family planned a camping trip. The children had been saving money for a long time. Now it was time to buy what they wanted to take with them.

So Peter, Janet, and Elaine started for town. They clutched their money carefully as they hurried along the path. Peter was eager to buy a map and compass. He meant to study the lay of the land at camp.

Late in the afternoon, all purchases made, the children made their way to an ice cream stand. They each had held onto enough money for a double-decker ice cream cone. "Mine's going to be pineapple," Peter said. "Oh, boy, I can hardly wait!"

"I wish we could take some to the others," Elaine said.

"Well, you know it would melt," Janet said. "So don't spoil our fun by thinking about it."

Three happy children stood, their backs to the wall next to the ice cream stand, licking their ice cream, when suddenly Elaine grabbed Peter's arm, making him drop his cone.

"Hey, Elaine, look what you're doing!" Peter began.

"Never mind your ice cream, Peter. Look! Look quick! Over there, Peter, over there!" Elaine pointed towards the corner where a man stood, ready to cross the street.

"What about 'over there'?" Peter wanted to know, looking longingly at his ice cream melting on the sidewalk.

Show Illustration #30

"It's him! It's the man I saw in the garden, Peter. I'd know him anywhere. Here, take my ice cream but keep looking. I'll hide in this doorway. I don't want him to see me."

But it was too late. Before Elaine could duck out of sight the man turned. He stared at her and it was plain to see he recognized her. Instead of waiting for the light to change, he dashed across the street dodging cars here and there. Peter took off after him.

"Come on!" he yelled, waving the ice cream cone high over his head. "Let's catch him!"

But the policeman on duty stopped the children. "Where do you think you're going dashing around in heavy traffic like this?" he demanded.

Show Illustration #31

Out of breath Peter stammered, "That man running up that side street. He's a burglar. Go get him, officer."

"I'm sorry," the policeman answered. "If he was the man who robbed the biggest bank, I couldn't leave my place here and follow him. But you go and report it to the police station. They may be able to do something about it."

"It's no use," Peter said, as in disappointment the children walked away. "The man saw you, Elaine, and he will hide for sure now. The police don't take much notice of children anyhow. We'll just go home and tell Dad about it."

"Yes, that's the best," Janet said. "Daddy can phone the police and tell them we've seen the man who broke into Philippa's house."

"One good thing," Elaine said. "Peter got a good look at him."

"Yup!" Peter swaggered, "I'd know that evil face anywhere now. If the police want help, all they need to do is call on detective Peter," and in a hurry he finished Elaine's ice cream cone–or what was left of it.

The next day the family left for camp. The car chugged up the steep hill to the cottage with Mr. Owen at the wheel. "Poor little old car may never make it up this hill," Mr. Owen laughed. "I may have to ask you to get out and push."

Show Illustration #32

There was a nice clearing on top of the hill and everyone hurried to put up tents and unroll the sleeping bags. In between they raced to the edge of the lake, longing to plunge in for a swim. Now and then a gull dipped and ruffled the surface of what otherwise looked to be a sheet of clear glass.

Late in the day everyone helped to build a big camp fire. Elaine thought food couldn't possibly taste better than the bacon and eggs Mrs. Owen showed them how to cook over the open fire. They couldn't wait for the potatoes to finish baking in the coals before they began to eat.

"Anyhow, baked potatoes make the most wonderful dessert," Mr. Owen declared. "We'll eat them a little later before we turn in for the night."

Everyone was ready to turn in early, weary from the excitement of the trip.

As the fire died down to glowing embers, Mr. Owen gathered the family around him and opened his Bible to read. Just below could be heard the soft bleating of sheep as Mr. Owen read, "And when He putteth forth His own sheep, He goeth before them, and the sheep follow Him: for they know His voice."

That night, when Elaine had curled up in her sleeping bag, she looked out the open flap of the tent and thought again of her verse. If the Lord had a special path of life for her to follow, she did hope it would always be with the Owens family. She had no desire to go back to her home in the city, even though she missed her mother at times.

Show Illustration #33

But the family worship around the camp fire had been about the Saviour-Shepherd, who went before His sheep. She was one of His sheep now. And the Bible said His sheep knew His voice.

"Help me, dear Lord, to be willing to follow the path of life You have chosen for me. Help me always to obey Your voice."

Dropping off to sleep, Elaine seemed to hear Mr. Owen again say what he had said before, "There is fullness of joy anywhere, if we are walking the path of life with Jesus."

She would try to remember this always.

Chapter 8

The next morning while Janet took her turn helping Mother, Peter and Elaine went exploring. Peter had his map and compass strapped to his back. "We can't get lost while I have these," he assured his mother.

But after they had been exploring a long time, a heavy fog came up from the lake and seemed to wrap around them like a blanket. They stood in the shelter of a jutting rock discussing which way the camp lay. Suddenly Peter exclaimed, "Look! There's a man coming down the path. I wonder who it could be?"

After he passed them, Elaine whispered, "It's him! Peter! It's the robber!"

"It's him all right," Peter answered. "Come on! Let's follow him. He can't hear us in our sneakers."

The man walked quickly and did not seem to know that Peter was right behind him. Elaine had to trot to keep up. She could not see Peter because of the fog. Then she stumbled over a clump of bushes and fell down flat. She was alone in a world of fog, a really frightened girl. When she got to her feet, she didn't know which way to go. If she couldn't find Peter, she'd have to find camp. She roamed 'round and 'round and on and on and on.

Show Illustration #34

Hours later the earth under her suddenly gave way and she slid down a bank. When she tried to get up, she could not. Her leg was very painful.

"Help!" Elaine shouted. "Someone, please help me!"

"Who's there?" The voice terrified her. Elaine saw the scowling face of the robber. She put her hands to her face and gave a little scream.

"Well, if it ain't the little girl of the garden," he said. "Now what are you doing here? Following me, eh? Get up!"

"I–I–can't," Elaine sobbed. "I can't walk. I think my leg is broken."

"Is that so?" the man said in a kinder voice. "Well, you don't have to be afraid. I won't hurt you. Here. Put your arms around my neck. I'll carry you inside."

Show Illustration #35

Elaine smelled whiskey on his breath and felt his unshaven face. Then darkness seemed to reach out and cover her. All night long the little girl lay, not knowing that kind hands were caring for her. If she could have seen the look in the man's face she would not have been afraid. "Such a little thing," he murmured. "And so much like my little Sally. I wonder where Sally is now? I hope someone is being kind to *her*."

Early the next morning Peter and Mr. Owen found them there–the man who could have escaped and left the girl alone, and the frightened child whose leg was dreadfully painful.

Before they carried Elaine back to camp, Mr. Owen had a long talk with the man. "You know that someday you'll be found," he said. "The police are looking for you all the time. Why not give yourself up? It will be better for you if you do."

Show Illustration #36

The man sat with head between his hands.

Mr. Owen continued, "I promise you that I'll stand by you. And you may be very sure I'll tell them how kind you've been to Elaine. Come on, what do you say?"

Feeling that he had found a friend at last, the man helped get Elaine back to camp. Leaving the family in Peter's care, Mr. Owen took Elaine to a hospital. Then he went with the burglar to the police station.

Elaine was a very sick girl for a long time. Not only was her leg broken, but she had pneumonia from the exposure in the damp woods. When the fever lessened and she was conscious, she saw her mother sitting beside her bed. "Hello, Mother," she said weakly.

Sobbing, Elaine's mother said, "My poor little girl. I'll never go off and leave you again. As soon as you are well, you will come back to the city with me and we shall always be together." She wondered why Elaine did not seem to be happy at this news.

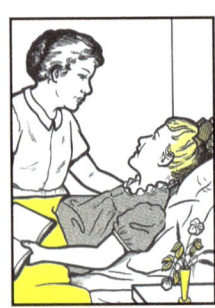

Show Illustration #37

Later Elaine talked to Mrs. Owen. "If only my mother could come and live with us here in the country," she said. "I'm sure she doesn't know what she's missing by living in the city all the time. I don't want to go back to the city to live."

"But your mother has her work there, Elaine. I'm afraid she would never be happy living here. She would miss the exciting times she loves. And remember, Elaine, your mother doesn't know about 'fullness of joy.' Perhaps this is the path of life the Lord now has for you. Of course, dear, I cannot decide these things for you. If your mother is willing, we'd certainly love to have you here with us, always."

Finally the day came when Elaine was allowed to leave the hospital. All the family waited to welcome her. *How different this is from the first time I came here,* Elaine thought. *How could I ever have been as mean and selfish as I was then?*

But wait a minute! Maybe I'm just as selfish now. I want to stay here always, when my mother really needs me.

Elaine shrugged off these thoughts as she smiled and waved to the children standing at the gate.

Show Illustration #38

They held a banner which read:

WELCOME HOME

Then everyone was talking at once. They told her the robber was in prison now, but Mr. Owen was visiting him regularly and that he had been able to lead him to the Lord. "And I have the promise of a job for him when he gets out," Mr. Owen said. "It won't be easy for the man. But he will have the Saviour with him now to help and guide him."

They had made a bed for Elaine downstairs. And that evening after everyone had gone out of the room to let her rest for a bit, the little girl looked out the window for a long time.

Show Illustration #39

The far hills seemed very near. On one of them she could see a lonely little path winding up over the rocks. It seemed to run right to the top and meet the sunset.

All that Elaine had learned about her verse came to her mind. "Thou wilt show me the path of life–the path that Jesus had planned for her. "In Thy presence"– traveling hand in hand with the Lord Jesus along that path–"is fullness of joy."

"Lord Jesus," Elaine whispered, "show me the path. I really want to know."

When Mother and Dad Owen and all the children gathered around Elaine's bed that evening for family worship, Mrs. Owen knew by the look on Elaine's face that the struggle was over.

"Did you find out, Elaine?" she whispered. "Is it the 'path of life' for you to return with your mother?"

Elaine nodded.

"Then you'll find 'fullness of joy.'"

Again Elaine nodded as the Bible reading began.

To be sung to the tune of the chorus of "Coming Again.")

Fullness of joy, fullness of joy.
When at work or when at play,
Christ is with me throughout each day.
Fullness of joy, fullness of joy.
He who has promised abundant life,
Has given me fullness of joy!

www.ingramcontent.com/pod-product-compliance
Lightning Source LLC
Chambersburg PA
CBHW042019150426
43197CB00002B/75